Brer Rabbit
at the Well

by Sharon Richards
illustrated by John Kurtz

 HOUGHTON MIFFLIN   BOSTON

Printed in China

ISBN-13: 978-0-547-02850-7
ISBN-10: 0-547-02850-4

6 7 8 9 0940 15 14 13 12
4500345288

The animals in the village
decided to plant a garden,
so they got some tools and seeds.
Brer Rabbit joined in.

Planting the garden was
hard work.
Brer Rabbit leaned on his hoe.
He was tired and wanted
to take a nap.
Then Brer Rabbit had an idea.
"Ow!" he cried.
"I have a thorn in my paw."

Hoe

"Pull out the thorn,"
said Brer Bear.
"Wash the cut at the well,"
said Brer Wolf.
Brer Rabbit tossed his hoe aside.
He went to the well to take a nap!
"Let the other animals work,"
thought Brer Rabbit.

Well

Brer Rabbit saw two buckets
hanging inside the well.
An empty bucket was at the top.
A bucket full of water was
at the bottom.

Bucket

Brer Rabbit jumped into the empty
bucket for a nap, but he was heavier
than the bucket of water.
He dropped to the bottom of
the well.

Brer Fox had followed Brer Rabbit
to the well.
He wanted to see if Brer Rabbit
was really washing his cut.

Brer Fox looked into the well.

"What are you doing down there?"
asked Brer Fox.

Brer Rabbit thought quickly.

"I'm fishing," he said.

Brer Fox jumped into the bucket
so he could fish, too.
His bucket went to the bottom,
and Brer Rabbit's bucket went
to the top.

Brer Rabbit jumped from his bucket
and ran back to the village.
Brer Fox had to wait until
a farmer came along.
The farmer pulled up the bucket
and was startled by what he saw.
Brer Fox jumped from the bucket
and ran home, too!

Farmer

Responding

✔ **TARGET SKILL** **Understanding Characters** What did you learn about Brer Rabbit and Brer Fox in the story? Copy and complete the chart below.

Character	Action	What It Means
Brer Rabbit	He says there's a thorn in his paw.	He can trick others.
Brer Fox	?	?

✎ Write About It

Text to Text What other stories have you read about characters who play tricks? Write a few sentences that tell how you feel about one of those characters. Give examples to support your ideas.

contained	search
grateful	startled
leaned	tossed
odd	village

TARGET SKILL **Understanding Characters** Tell more about the characters.

TARGET STRATEGY **Summarize** Stop to tell important events as you read.

GENRE A **folktale** is a story that is often told by people of a country.